W9-AVM-313

Colossal and Concrete

What Am I?

by Joyce Markovics

Consultant: Eric Darton, Adjunct Faculty
New York University Urban Design and Architecture Studies Program
New York, New York

T 19830

BEARPORT
PUBLISHING

New York, New York

Credits

Cover, © aragami12345s/Shutterstock; 2 © Oscity/Shutterstock; TOC, © Sfeichtner/Shutterstock; 4–5, © Bildagentur-online/Schickert/Alamy; 6–7, © Oscity/Shutterstock; 8–9, © Jim Parkin/Alamy; 10–11, © Steve Buckley/Shutterstock; 12–13, © James Steidl/Shutterstock; 14–15, © David R. Frazier Photolibrary, Inc./Alamy; 16–17, © Sfeichtner/Shutterstock; 18–19, © Andrew Zarivny/Shutterstock; 20–21, © Andrew Zarivny/Shutterstock; 22, © robert cicchetti/Shutterstock; 23, © GL Archive/Alamy; 24, © Douglas Rial/iStock.

Publisher: Kenn Goin
Senior Editor: Joyce Tavolacci
Creative Director: Spencer Brinker
Design: Debrah Kaiser

Library of Congress Cataloging-in-Publication Data

Names: Markovics, Joyce L., author.
Title: Colossal and concrete : what am I? / by Joyce Markovics.
Description: New York, New York : Bearport, [2018] | Series: American place
  puzzlers | Includes bibliographical references and index.
Identifiers: LCCN 2017039492 (print) | LCCN 2017042409 (ebook) |
ISBN 9781684025398 (ebook) | ISBN 9781684024810 (library)
Subjects: LCSH: Hoover Dam (Ariz. and Nev.)—Juvenile literature.
Classification: LCC TC557.5.H6 (ebook) | LCC TC557.5.H6 M37 2018 (print) |
  DDC 627/.80979159—dc23
LC record available at https://lccn.loc.gov/2017039492

For more information, write to Bearport Publishing Company, Inc., 45 West 21st Street, Suite 3B, New York, New York 10010. Printed in the United States of America.

10 9 8 7 6 5 4 3 2 1

Contents

What Am I?

I am made
of colossal
concrete blocks.

4

Each one is 5 feet
(1.5 m) tall!

I sit in a huge,
rocky canyon.

6

There is a
road on top of me.

8

There are
four towers
alongside me.

10

Water flows into
each one.

I have special machines.

12

They help
make electricity.

Millions of
people visit
me each year.

14

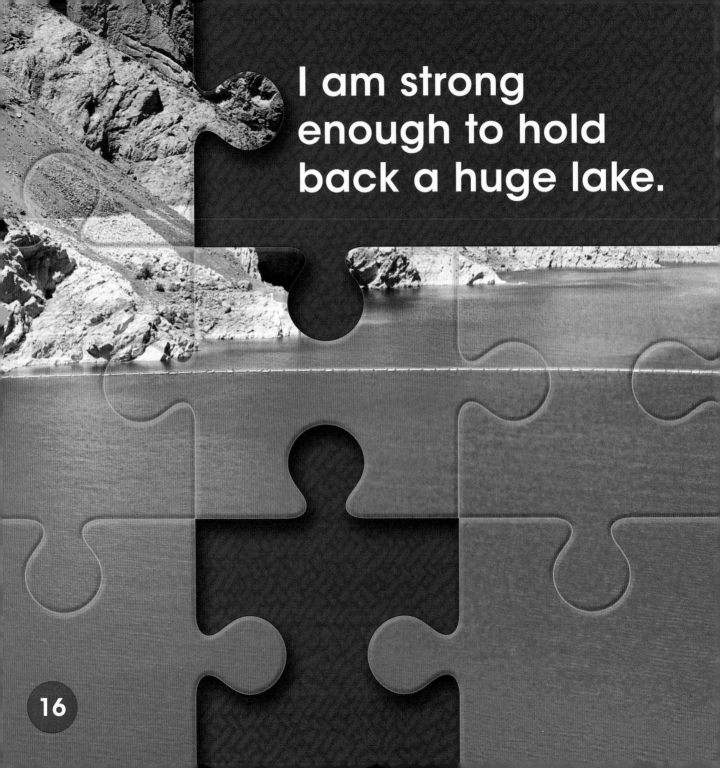

I am strong enough to hold back a huge lake.

16

What am I?

Let's find out!

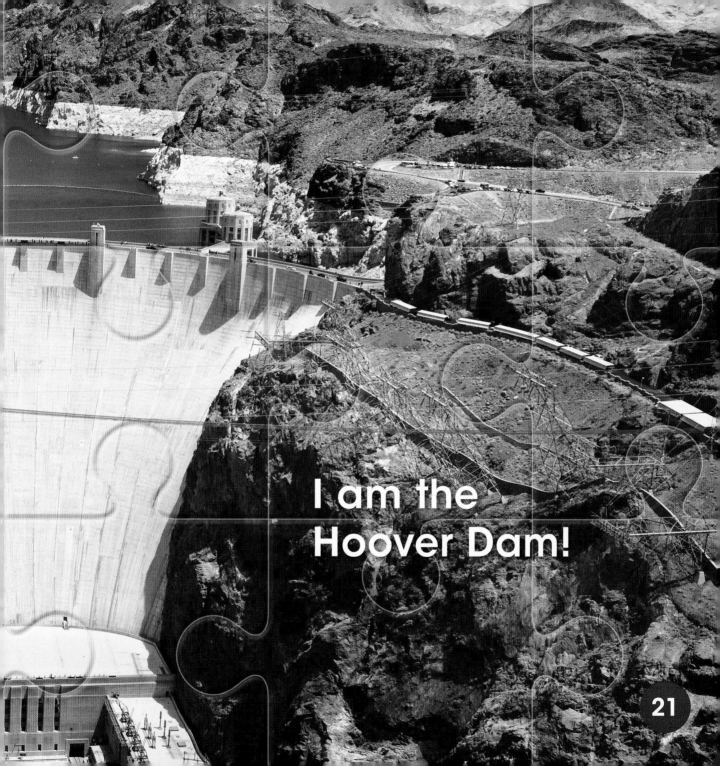

I am the
Hoover Dam!

Fast Facts

The Hoover Dam is a huge concrete dam. It was built between 1931 and 1936. At that time, it was the biggest dam in the world!

The Hoover Dam

Height:	726 feet (221 m)
Width:	1,244 feet (379 m)
Thickness at Top:	45 feet (14 m)
Thickness at Bottom:	660 feet (201 m)
Weight:	6.6 million tons (6 mt)
Cool Fact:	Each year, the Hoover Dam provides electricity for about 8 million people.

Where Am I?

The Hoover Dam is located in the Black Canyon of the Colorado River. It sits on the border between Nevada and Arizona.

CANADA

Pacific Ocean

N
W   E
S

UNITED STATES OF AMERICA

Atlantic Ocean

MEXICO

NEVADA

Hoover Dam

ARIZONA

The Hoover Dam is named after former President Herbert Hoover.

Index

Read More

Murray, Julie. *Hoover Dam (All Aboard America).* North Mankato, MN: Buddy Books (2005).

Zuehkle, Jeffrey. *The Hoover Dam (Lightning Bolt Books: Famous Places).* Minneapolis, MN: Learner (2010).

Learn More Online

To learn more about the Hoover Dam, visit
www.bearportpublishing.com/AmericanPlacePuzzlers

About the Author

Joyce Markovics lives in a very old house along the Hudson River, not far from the New Croton Dam.